A Beginner's Guide to Water Gardens

Gardening Series

Dueep Jyot Singh

Mendon Cottage Books

JD-Biz Publishing

Disclaimer

The information is this book is provided for informational purposes only. It is not intended to be used and medical advice or a substitute for proper medical treatment by a qualified health care provider. The information is believed to be accurate as presented based on research by the author.

The contents have not been evaluated by the U.S. Food and Drug Administration or any other Government or Health Organization and the contents in this book are not to be used to treat cure or prevent disease.

The author or publisher is not responsible for the use or safety of any diet, procedure or treatment mentioned in this book. The author or publisher is not responsible for errors or omissions that may exist.

Warning

The Book is for informational purposes only and before taking on any diet, treatment or medical procedure, it is recommended to consult with your primary health care provider.

Check out some of the other Healthy Gardening Series books at Amazon.com

Gardening Series on Amazon

Check out some of the other Health Learning Series books at Amazon.com

Health Learning Series on Amazon

Table of Contents

Introduction

I was talking about gardening with a friend, who is an avid gardener, when we got onto the topic of water Gardens. Her immediate reaction was "how do you make a water garden in a limited space, especially in congested cities. Water gardens are only for those houses built in really wide-open spaces, and plenty of land where you can go high, wide and free, making a water garden."

Unfortunately, that is the mindset of a number of people out there, who are under the impression that you need plenty of land in which to make a water garden. That is because the moment you say this word water garden, you visualize a huge pool, in which a number of exotic plant species float.

You may also find some Koi goldfish moving leisurely to and fro, and people appreciating that garden while walking around it leisurely of an evening.

Well, that may be all right for a hotel lobby, where no expenses are spared. However, ordinary water gardens can be made right in your back yard, in the limited space, and with a little bit of creative gardening. I told my friend that a water garden could be made in the amount of space, in which she wanted to erect a water fountain, and she blinked.

What is the fun of a small water garden was her immediate response. I replied, "Just think about it. After all, you are planting some attractive plant species which are growing in water. This is a contrast to the plants growing on land. You do not have any kids, and you do not have any pets which may find them taking a ducking in that water garden. So think about it. "

She did. And now she has a small water garden in her backyard. It has water lilies and lotuses goldfish and even tadpoles in it. Also a Walt Disney statue of Snow white's pal Dopey looking at his reflection in his typical dopey fashion.

The idea of water gardening is definitely not a modern concept. Since millenniums, water gardens have been a part of garden layouts. Be they the palaces of Caesar, in Greece, or a castle in Spain, or a manor in Britain or perhaps the palace of Kublai Khan, you could be certain that there would be a water garden built there, and tended carefully and lovingly by all the gardeners.

Water lilies are among the best-known of aquatic plants, grown in a water garden. They grow to various sizes and are suitable for all types of pools.

That is because water adds charm to a garden. It is easy to manage water content, and it is ever-changing. It also blends effectively with rocks and plants.

One of the Seven Wonders Of The Ancient World, the hanging Gardens of Assyria – the idea that they were situated in Babylon is a fallacy – definitely had water gardens. Apart from lotuses and water lilies, they would have a number of exotic aquatic plants, making the garden a thing of beauty and a joy forever.

Growing Plants in Your Water Garden

Many beautiful and unusual plants can be grown in a water garden, and the making of such a garden is an adventure within the reach of everyone, even if he is a beginner to the idea of gardening.

That is because almost any container or receptacle, which is capable of holding water is a potential pool! Believe it or not, there are water lilies which are small enough to live and flourish in an ordinary sized washing up bowl. There you are, you have a small miniature water garden in the making!

In fact, it is not necessary for you to look for lots of space, to build your water garden, especially when you are strapped for space in a flat.

If your water garden is well constructed, if care is taken with the planting, and if the right planting compost material and aquatic plants are chosen, water is easier to manage than grass. However, you are going to take great care to hold a balance between Clear water and a well-managed pool and smelly, slimy green water and rank aquatic plants growing in an unattractive pool.

Here is the difference between success and failure.

Siting Your Pool

The position of water in a garden is very important because water lilies and most aquatic plants love the sun. So if you are living in a climate, where the sun does not appear for long stretches of time, you may find it difficult to make a water lily garden or pool.

Formal and Informal Water Gardens

Water gardens are either formal or informal and should fit in with their surroundings.

No lilies here in the château of Versailles formal gardens water fountain , but the statues are there.

The former water garden is usually the dominant feature of a garden – in the central position or perhaps the focus point of any area to which all the paths are going to lead. It is going to be irregular in shape, either a circle, square, oblong or some geometric form.

The outline of a formal garden is defined with the raised paved surround. Fountains can also be placed in water gardens, but as a general rule, running water is not desirable in my opinion, first because of the wastage of water. Also, if you are getting this water from a natural spring or similar low-lying source of water, it is going to lower the temperature constantly. That means your water lilies are definitely not going to be happy in this cold water.

Formal pools look better in conventional surroundings, and do not blend with natural features such as wild or rock gardens or Alpine meadows. Keep the vegetation in them low, using water lilies and submerged and floating aquatic plants rather than bog plants or marginal plants.

Informal pools should not show their origin. Concrete and other materials, which make up an informal pool should be hidden by keeping the outer edges below the level of the surrounding ground and by the skillful use of marginal plants. These marginal plants can be bog plants. These are going to bridge the gap between the water and the dry land.

The informal pool blends with any natural setting, and is therefore not the best type of pool for a formal garden, or similarly strictly tailored garden.

There are different types of pools, which have grown popular down the ages. A **classical pool** is going to be made up of carefully chosen stone flags, to make the effect of a severely classical formal pool.

The cornerstones provide ideal stands for tubs and large plants such as *Agapanthus* and shrubs such as Bay trees. These classical pools were very popular during ancient times in Egypt, Greece and Rome, when system and methodology was everything, even in designing a garden.

Interesting reflections – now, this is the type of garden which you may find in a traditional Japanese Zen garden. We are going to find reflections of plants in the water, which are going to add interest to the garden.

Stone Figures like statues of mythical animals or human figurines are placed at the edge which is going to be mirrored effectively when there are no plants to break the image.

Miniature water gardens are going to be made of any strong containers, especially when you have stone troughs. You can plant one or two lilies, according to the size of the trough. The rocks that formed the firm base can be inter—planted with rock plants like *Dianthus*.

Statues and stone carvings among reeds can also be made by a number of reed plants, edged with water lilies.

A paved garden, like a classic design can be made as the centerpiece of your garden. This may have an irregular outline to relieve the former severity of the stone paving.

The warmer the water, the more luxuriant the plant growth and the greater the number of blooms you are going to have. That is why water lily gardens flourished in tropical areas, and Mediterranean areas, and also in hot areas like Egypt.

Water lily ponds in ancient classical lands still bring forth seeds, which have been buried in the silt for 2000 years, and which have been excavated, and which still manage to grow when planted in the Kew gardens.

This shows that the instinct to survive in these plants is very strong, and they are going to lie dormant, if the conditions are inclement. But the moment the conditions are fine, they are going to rise and shine and Bloom and grow.

A pool should therefore be built in the open as far as possible, in the fresh sun and air.

The shelter of trees or a hedge to the windy side of a water garden is going to break the force of possible winds and considerably extends the flowering season.

But be sure to build the pool some distance from the trees or hedges so that you do not have dead leaves falling into the tool and fouling the water.

Alternatively, you can spread wire netting over the surface of the pool during the first few weeks of the autumn fall.

Shallow Pools or Deep Pools?

A very deep pool can be a disadvantage because depth controls the temperature of the water, but the water must not be too shallow or it is going to freeze up in the winter. 15 to 18 inches of water above the crowns of the plants is shallow enough to induce free flowering. It is also sufficiently deep to safeguard the roots of your plants in the winter.

Rock garden pools are open only about 1 feet or even less in depth, and they should be protected during a very bad winter. But such a precaution is going to be hard to practice for larger pools.

Different Types of Pools

Normally, there are four principal types of pool constructions for a gardener to choose from. You can make the pool in concrete. You can also fit pre-shaped pools made of plastic materials such as fiberglass. You can adapt old containers such as barrels, tabs and baths. Or you can line an excavation with sheeting and make a water retainer and container.

Concrete Pools

These are the most popular, especially when you want something long-term. That is because the material is so flexible, and can be made in any shape or size. A concrete pool does not need to be the same depth all over. You can make a shallow part in one end, to reduce the cost and labor of the excavation and because of its shallowness, it will make it easier to shape the surrounding part, which can be as deep as required.

In short, that the pool is watertight. That means that the water is not going to be absorbed in the soil slowly and steadily.

How to Make Your Own Pond

Here is an easy way in which you can make your own pond, by excavating the soil to a death of three feet. This allows for 6 inches of concrete, 6 inches of soil or the depth of a basket and one and a half feet of water and some more. That is after you have marked out the deep area with pegs.

A rectangular tank is easy as to construct. Make sure the base is level and free of loose soil before laying the concrete. This should be spread over the whole floor of the pool in just one operation. Roughen the edges for about 6 inches all around with a trowel. This is to make a key for the new concrete when you are constructing the sides.

These sites can be built in a variety of ways. For instance, you can use a brick wall and then cover it in concrete. But perhaps the most efficient method is to construct a roofless and bottomless box of stout timber to stand inside the excavation with about 6 inches to spare all around, and then to pack concrete into the space in between the earth and the wood.

Build up the necessary depth of cement by working continuously around the box. Do not complete one side at a time. Take special care to force the material down at the corners.

Oiling or soft soaping the board beforehand makes it easier to remove them a few days later when the concrete has set.

The outer rim of the pool is thus made in the same way, except that it is only necessary to escalate about 10 inches of soil. You are allowing for 4 inches of concrete and 6 inches of water. Sides 4 inches thick, will be strong enough for this part of the pool.

As it is important that the pool be waterproof, used only top-quality materials like Portland cement, coarse sand, and clean gravel. Aggregate if used, should be of varying sizes between ¾ inches and 3/18 inches.

They should be mixed in the proportions of one cement, two parts sand, and three parts clean gravel or aggregate with sufficient water to make a good stiff dough.

If you think mixing concrete is too hard a business, it is worth considering the use of ready mixed concrete. Allow the concrete to mature before you allow water to be stored in this container.

Prefabricated Pools

They are made of fiberglass or aluminum and are so light that even a child can handle them. All you have to do to install these pools is to excavate a hole in which they just fit. You are going to be provided with a template with them. Check the rim for level, and allow water to flow into this container. Ask your nursery professional, if he has this pool in sizes suitable for your garden.

Miscellaneous Containers

You can either construct containers, or just use the ones which you have handy.

Bathtubs, stone troughs, and even galvanized tanks are excellent for storing water. You can use beer casks, and old wooden wine casks sawn into half. They can either be standing free with the outlet of the water pipe pouring the water into the cask or you can sink them in a hole, below ground level.

Most of these receptacles look good, when you have sunk them into the ground. If the rims are well below ground level, pieces of stone can be placed around the edges to mask the outlines.

I was thinking about polythene to waterproof these containers. I found out that these will not work very well in the hot sun, because then these sheets become thin and start to leak, especially in the rim area and when the pool is full.

Polythene Sheeting

This is a cheap and simple method of preparing a site for growing aquatics. All you need is to excavate an area so that you can get the required shape and line the depression with thick polythene sheeting. 500 gauge sheeting is best, and all you have to do after lining is to fill with water and introduce the plants. These plans will be in baskets. Also, you can keep fish in such ponds.

This URL can give you information about plastic sheeting, which is friendly to aquatic plants and fish.

http://www.globalplasticsheeting.com/aquaponics-plastic-film/

This sheeting expands so that when you slowly fill with water, it is going to take up the exact shape of the excavation. It is available in a variety of colors and has greater strength than ordinary polythene.

The only source of danger to such sheeting is that exposure to anything sharp is going to spell disaster. Also, if the hot sun constantly plays on the material above the waterline, it is going to leak. So protect the edges of these plastic pools with pieces of rock or by laying soil or paving stones up to the edge of the water and keep them always full of water.

Stream Gardens

Rock and water are natural partners and in the garden, streams and waterfalls not only bring beauty, but sound and movement as well. A large area of ground is not essential but the site must of course be sloping.

At the highest point, water from a hidden or source is going to trickle slowly into the basin or cavity. It is then going to spill over in a waterfall or collect in another basin.

Here it is going to spill over again before running via a stream to the largest area of water, which is your proper pool.

Surprisingly, little water is needed to create these attractive effects, and there are several models of small water pumps in the market which will return the water so that you can use them over and over again.

Remember that water which is moving constantly is not good for lilies and the more decorative aquatic plants, so that the source of supply should be turned off at night and in cold weather.

Also, the path of the water from the top of the rock garden to the main pool should not be too straight. That is because in nature, water takes the line of least resistance, finding its way through soft rock and round obstacles in steady descent to the lowest reaches.

You may want to visit a formal or informal garden, to see how the experienced gardeners have set out their Stream Gardens.

Bog Gardens

There are many plants which like feeling the influence of water around them without really growing in it. They cannot stand drought. Also, they cannot live in stagnant moisture. These are the bog plants, many of which are the most colorful plants in your water garden.

There are several alternative ways of arranging these plants for constant moisture during the active growing season. Firstly, the area can be flooded periodically, which is quite successful if the floodwater is trapped.

But if it runs all over the garden, it is going to be a waste and a nuisance. Especially if you are practicing sustainable gardening. There is also a danger that, during the period of summer and draught, when water is most urgently required, local authorities may enforce water restrictions

Been there seen that. Is it worth making a garden under such circumstances where you need so much water?

Here is one extremely easy- to- implement solution. Place 6 inches of drainage material such as broken rocks, clinker, and stones over the base of a 1 feet deep basin. Cover this with a layer of turf –grass side downward – and then 10 to 12 inches of compost. In this soil bed, raised above the level of the neighboring pool, you are going to have the crown of the plant resting securely. At the same time, the plant roots will go down to and feel the influence of the water below.

Often there is no need to carry out any special construction work to grow bog plants. They are going to flourish in reasonably moist or heavy soil with sufficient moisture is present in the ground to take care of their needs.

You may want to give them an annual top dressing with a mulch of well composted and rotting leaves in early May or in the beginning of spring. This is going to conserve the moisture.

Using a Tub as a Water Garden

Just imagine that you have a tub, and it is serving no useful purpose. You can make a pool with this container by sinking it into the ground so that the plants can be seen from above. If the rims are well below ground, give the pool decorative edges by placing pieces of stone or scrambling plants around the edges.

The soil inside the containers can be built up round rocks to give the required depth.

Planting in Containers

Baskets are ideal containers for water lilies, so that the Lily crowns [crowns – the parts of the plants, which are above the soil and which include stem, leaves, flowers, seeds and branches.] are just above the water. If you do not have containers, you can place the bricks on the bottom of the pool before it is filled with water.

Leave spaces between the bricks for the water to seep through.

Winter Care of Pools

During the winter months, keep the garden pools full of water as this is the best insurance against frost damage to plants and fish.

Cover very shallow pools during sustained cold spells. Prefabricated pools are often sold with mats for this purpose, but you can use boards or branches laid across the surface and covered with sacks. These are equally effective.

Remove the coverings as soon as the thaw sets in, or premature growth will take place in the warmth engendered beneath them.

If possible keep a hole open in the pool to give fresh air to any fish. Do not banged up on the ice with a heavy hammer as this is going to injure both your fish and the concrete. Allow a ball or piece of wood to float on the surface and lift this out every day so that the ice ground it can be chipped gently.

In the autumn, and before you leave the garden for the winter, cut all the herbage asked the waterside as low as possible to prevent it from harboring the larvae of water lily beetles and other pests. Also remove all the dead leaves and debris from the water lilies and from the pond as far as possible. This rotting down of this kind of debris is the chief reason for cloudy pools.

Planting Your Pools

Water lilies, Aponogetons and Nuphars are really hearty feeders and need a good, rich planting compost. Do not economize on this planting compost because is going to result in the paucity of blooms, small stunted leaves and a general meagerness of growth.

These plants need good heavy loam, such as the top soil from pastureland, which has rotted down for 6 to 9 month. You can also use clay soil, which has been enriched with decayed cow manure-1/6 of its bulk – for at least 12 months. You can store this soil under cover to prevent the destruction of its mineral properties by exposure to sun and rain.

Other natural manures are unsuitable.

If you cannot get cow manure the best substitute is coarse bone meal used in the proportion of a 5 inch pot full to a barrel full load of soil.

Mix the constituents together thoroughly, remove any fibrous material, and if necessary, water this heap to get it into a moist condition.

No Organic Materials!

Do not introduce any of the organic materials normally associated with potting compost. This includes rotted compost, leaf mold, spent hops, Peat, and similar substances. This may make good food, but during that break down, they are going to charge the water with mineral salts. This is going to encourage algae, which is going to discolor your water.

Also, if there is too much organic matter in your water, putrid gases escape – this can sometimes be seen bubbling upwards throughout the water and suffocate your fish.

Growing Water Lilies

There are two popular methods of growing water lilies in artificial pools. One is to place a five – 6 inch carpet of prepared loam across the base of the empty pool and plant directly into this material. The disadvantage of this method is that when it is time to attend to or lift and divide the plants, the gardener needs to churn up all the mud and the water loses its clarity that is one of its chief attractions.

If you are planting by this method, make sure that the soil is in a moist and even sticky condition. This ensures firm planting because dry soil does not bind effectively, and once the water has been added to it, the roots often become dislodged and float.

Plant according to the root stocks. Place the lilies with the rhizomes horizontally and set firmly with the growing points of the shoots just protruding from the soil. Barely cover the top of the rhizome with the soil.

Other plant types which have a root somewhat like celery should be planted up to the collar with the roots going straight down into the soil. The "collar" is that visible portion of the plant, with a soil mark on it showing you how deeply it was planted when you got that plant from the nursery. That soil mark is going to be on the stem of your growing plant.

The second method is to plant the water lilies directly into containers. This can be done by using galvanized wire or wicker baskets or even wooden slats or concrete boxes.

Although these are not so long-lasting as other containers, baskets are the best option, because the open sides allow the water content to come into contact with the soil. If you use boxes of wood or concrete, bore holes in the sides and base beforehand.

Firm planting is even more essential for this method. Otherwise the planting is the same as for the first method. Leave sufficient room in the basket to top dress the soil with shingle.

This is going to prevent the fish from disturbing the mud and fouling the water.

Maintenance and Care

When planting by the first method is finished, run in just enough of water to cover the crowns of the lilies. After a few days, run in another couple of inches, and continue in this way until your pool is quite full.

This is a worthwhile procedure because the water lilies have sustained the shock of transplantation by then. They do not want this shock aggravated by the running in of a large bulk of cold water, possibly straight from the tap.

If the water is added in direct ratio to their growth, the lilies are going to develop gradually and will probably flower in the first season.

When the lilies are planted in baskets or containers, fill up the pool first. This should be done some days previously. Raise the baskets on bricks, so that the crowns of the lilies stand just below water level. As the growth proceeds, lower these platforms gradually until the baskets are eventually standing on the concrete base of the pool.

Cleaning Your Pond

From time to time, small plants need to be replanted after you have emptied out the pool and cleaned it. That is because the lilies may have exhausted the soil and the flowers will have become fewer and smaller.

Most of the plants will need drastic division. Empty the pool and rinse it. Put the plants in fresh soil like you did before. Now plant your plants.

Planting Aquatic Plants

You do not need stimulants for aquatic plants that grow at the margin of your pool. The only problem is going to be – keeping them compact and within bounds. Use plain, heavy, fibreless loam in shallow troughs and plant directly into these.

Floating aquatic plants are simply placed on the water surface.

Planting Oxygenators

Oxygenators are those plants which promote the presence of oxygen in the water. One oxygenator should be allowed to every square foot of water. These submerged oxygenators have small rootstocks and in soil bottomed pools, you need to weigh them with strips of zinc and drop them into place. They are soon going to form their own roots for anchorage.

Pools without any soil need to have oxygenators introduced in the same way as the lilies – in containers. You will fill shallow pans or boxes and a little charcoal and insert these plants as cuttings. This is the simplest way to plant them, and they soon settle in, when the containers have been dropped into place.

Best Planting Time

Springtime, especially from March until the beginning of June is the best time for planting water lilies and stronger aquatic plants, but oxygenators and floaters can be introduced at any time during the summer months. Plant the bog plants, either in early autumn or early spring.

Livestock in Your Pool

The added livestock not only adds to the attractiveness of the pool, but it also makes a balanced community. Fishes and water snails feed on the insect and debris. They fertilize the plants with their waste. The carbon dioxide that they exhale provide the underwater plants particularly with one of the necessary ingredients for photosynthesis.

This is the making of food and in turn, the release of oxygen during this vital procedure serves the need of respiration in both plants and animals.

Fishes also keep down many enemies. In their ceaseless search for food, they destroy aphids, mosquito larvae and other pests, and also bring color and movement to your water garden.

Surface swimming fish are the only ones suitable for an ornamental pool, but do not introduce them until six or eight weeks after planting has been completed.

Of this goldfish are the best varieties and will live in harmony together.

Other fish species like mirror carp, feed near the bottom of the pool and keep the water in a continuously cloudy condition by their constant foraging in the mud. So do not put them in your own pool.

Do not overstock your pool with fish, because if there is plenty of submerged vegetation, they are going to breed and multiply. You can ask any dealer in fish to advise you on the number required for a specific pool.

Artificial feeding is seldom necessary in an outdoor pool and in any case should not be overdone. Several times a week, you can give the fish as much food as they can consume in five minutes. If too much is provided, it is going to drop to the bottom and will start to ferment.

From November until March, stop artificial feeding entirely, because the water is too cold for the fish to digest the food properly and various ailments are going to follow unwise feeding or overfeeding of your fish.

Since goldfish normally exist in the winter on the fat content which is stored in their bodies, protein foods such as minced and raw meat, minced hard-boiled egg, or chopped earthworms can be given to them regularly between September and November to build up their constitutions for the winter fast.

Discolored Water

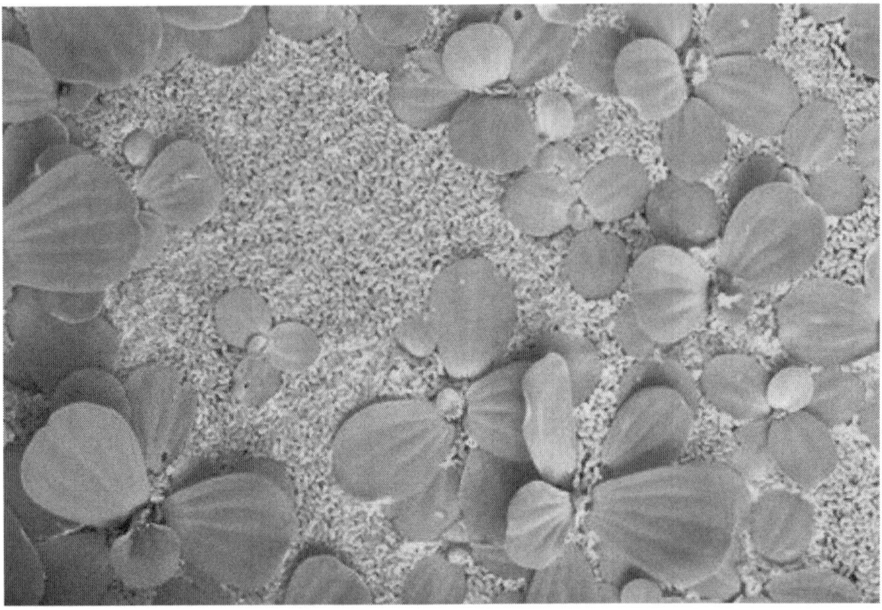

Weeds spoil the looks of your pond.

Green or cloudy water is the chief worry of a pool owner. It is caused by stirring up mud or sediment, or by microscopic plant life.

This green water owes this color to algae which are tiny plants. These appear from airborne spores and are going to multiply at a huge rate when the weather is sunny and the water contains lots of mineral salts.

To combat the algae, cut down supplies of both Sun and mineral salts. This can be done effectively by

- Adding no organic matter to the original planting compost.
- Removing all the rotting vegetable materials such as dead leaves and flowers regularly.
- Providing competition for the food in the pool by introducing more plants.

- Providing natural shade by adding floating plants such as water lilies and other surface aquatic plants.

A lot of plants covering the surface are going to discourage aquatic algae growth.

Floodwater from clay and silt is also going to cause discoloration, but the emptying and refilling of the pond from the tap is definitely no remedy. That is because the water available to you in the cities is treated with chlorine, and is not healthy, natural water. This is not pure either.

It is going to take time for the effect of these chemicals to wear off and for the water to take on that limpid appearance, which is found in a natural lake. Even the latter is subject to periodic bouts of cloudiness, usually in spring, but this soon settles.

Patience is the water gardener's best ally. In time, the pool will clear, although it may take up to 12 months to do so.

Some forms of algae are stronger and more tenacious than others, forming slimy bundles or hair like growths which are called blanket weeds.

These have to be removed by hand using the fingers or a twisted stick, which can be turned round and round and so you can wind up the blanket weed on the fingers or the stick from which it can later be removed.

This is a somewhat arduous process, but regular attention in the initial stages can keep the algae down.

Do not use chemical methods of weed control and is going to change the nature of the water and introduce other problems. Any poison capable of destroying algae can also affect your plants adversely.

Suggested Plants for Your Pool

Apart from water lilies, you can use other ornamental aquatics like *Acorus*– Sweet Flag ,*Alisma* – Water Plantains , *Aponogeton* – Water Hawthorne , *Butomus* – Flowering Rush, *Calla* – Bog Arum , *Caltha* – Marsh Marigold , Cotula – brass buttons, *Decodon* – Water Willow, *Echinodorus* , *Glyceria* – Manna Grass , *Iris, Juncus* – Rushes , *Jussieua* – Water Primrose , *Menyanthes* – Bog Bean , *Myosotis* – Forget Me Not , *Nuphar* – Spatterdock , *Sagittaria* and Ranunculus etc.

Floating plants include duckweed, water hyacinths, and water chestnuts.

Submerged aquatics good for oxygenation include American pond weed – *Anacharis*, Water Violets- *Hottonia*, water Crowfoot – Ranunculus, etc.

You can get an excellent list of the best aquatic plants for pools on this URL.

Even though this is a megastore, they have done an excellent job in collecting photographs of different aquatic plants, which can add distinction to your water garden.

https://www.pondmegastore.com/shop/home.php

Pick up the ones you want, and buy them from your nearest nursery.

Conclusion

I am sure you enjoyed the beginner's guide to water gardens. Not only are you going to enjoy a brand-new hobby when you make your own garden, but you have something which is going to add to the style quotient of your garden for years and years.

Check out some of the other Healthy Gardening Series books at Amazon.com

Gardening Series on Amazon

If you do not want to make a water garden, you can make a miniature garden with instructions given in my other books. –

Author Bio-

Dueep Jyot Singh is a Management and IT Professional who managed to gather Postgraduate qualifications in Management and English and Degrees in Science, French and Education while pursuing different enjoyable career options like being an hospital administrator, IT,SEO and HRD Database Manager/ trainer, movie , radio and TV scriptwriter, theatre artiste and public speaker, lecturer in French, Marketing and Advertising, ex-Editor of Hearts On Fire (now known as Solstice) Books Missouri USA, advice columnist and cartoonist, publisher and Aviation School trainer, ex- moderator on Medico.in, banker, student councilor ,travelogue writer … among other things!

One fine morning, she decided that she had enough of killing herself by Degrees and went back to her first love -- writing. It's more enjoyable! She already has 48 published academic and 14 fiction- in- different- genre books under her belt.

When she is not designing websites or making Graphic design illustrations for clients , she is browsing through old bookshops hunting for treasures, of which she has an enviable collection – including R.L. Stevenson, O.Henry, Dornford Yates, Maurice Walsh, De Maupassant, Victor Hugo, Sapper, C.N. Williamson, "Bartimeus" and the crown of her collection- Dickens "The Old Curiosity Shop," and so on… Just call her "Renaissance Woman") - collecting herbal remedies, acting like Universal Helping Hand/Agony Aunt, or escaping to her dear mountains for a bit of exploring, collecting herbs and plants and trekking.

Check out some of the other JD-Biz Publishing books

Gardening Series on Amazon

Health Learning Series

GRANDMA'S
NATURAL REMEDIES AND ANCIENT HERBAL BEAUTY RECIPES
Volume 1
HEALTH LEARNING SERIES
DUEEP J SINGH AND J DAVIDSON
GRANDMA'S
NATURAL REMEDIES AND ANCIENT HERBAL BEAUTY RECIPES
Volume 2
HEALTH LEARNING SERIES
DUEEP J SINGH AND J DAVIDSON
GRANDMA'S
NATURAL REMEDIES AND ANCIENT RECIPES
GRANDMA'S CURE FOR OBESITY
GRANDMA'S CURE FOR THE COMMON COLD
Volume 3
HEALTH LEARNING SERIES
DUEEP J SINGH AND J DAVIDSON
GRANDMA'S
NATURAL REMEDIES AND ANCIENT HERBAL RECIPES
Volume 4
HEALTH LEARNING SERIES
DUEEP J SINGH AND J DAVIDSON
GRANDMA'S
HERBAL LORE
ANCIENT HERBAL RECIPES AND REMEDIES
Volume 5
HEALTH LEARNING SERIES
DUEEP J SINGH AND J DAVIDSON
GRANDMA'S
ANCIENT BEAUTY REMEDIES FROM HER KITCHEN
Volume 6
HEALTH LEARNING SERIES
DUEEP J SINGH AND J DAVIDSON
GRANDMA'S
EASY TO USE TIPS
IN THE KITCHEN AND OUTDOORS
Volume 7
HEALTH LEARNING SERIES
DUEEP J SINGH AND J DAVIDSON
GRANDMA'S
HOUSEHOLD HINTS AND RECIPES
USING TIME TESTED ECONOMICAL TIPS IN YOUR HOME
75 Tips
Remove Stains
Peel Tomatoes
Perfect Pies
HEALTH LEARNING SERIES
DUEEP J SINGH AND J DAVIDSON
GRANDMA'S
NATURAL REMEDIES AND ANCIENT RECIPES
ALL 5 BOOKS IN 1
HEALTH LEARNING SERIES
DUEEP J SINGH AND J DAVIDSON

Amazing Health Benefits of Intermittent Fasting
What Makes Me Fat?
How to eliminate obesity naturally!
Natural Cures of Anxiety
Medical Conditions Requiring Paleo Diet
How to Eliminate Heart Burn and Acid Reflux Naturally
Eliminate Pain!
How to get rid of arthritis and joint pain naturally!
Ways to Improve Self-Esteem
Self esteem
How to Avoid Brain Aging Dementia - Memory Loss Naturally
Paleo Diet Side Effects
Paleo Diet
Good or Bad?
An Analysis of Arguments and Counter-Arguments
How to Get Rid of High Blood Pressure or Hypertension Naturally
Health Benefits of Meditation
Paleo Diet For Weight Loss
Paleo Diet for Athletes
How to Reduce the Chances of a Heart Attack
How to Get Rid of Asthma Naturally
By M Usman and J Davidson

Amazing Animal Book Series

Learn To Draw Series

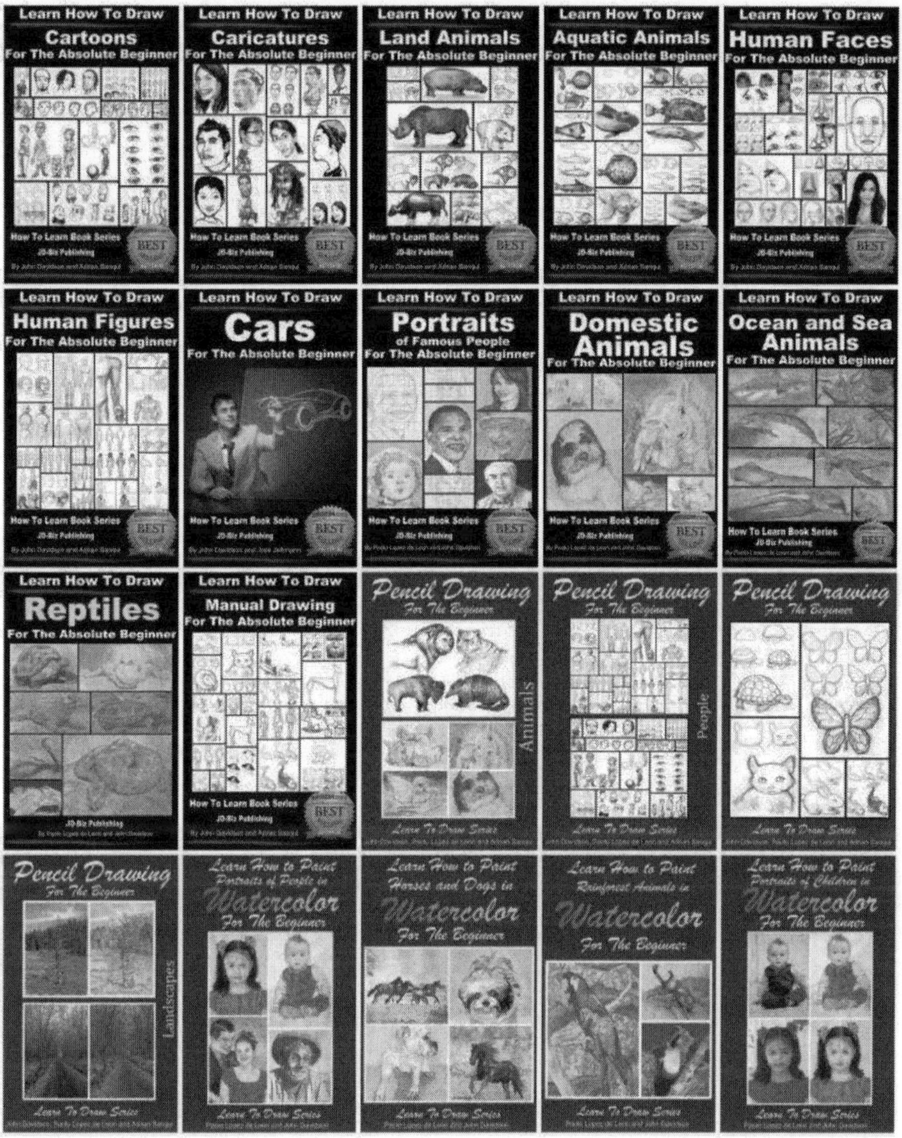

How to Build and Plan Books

Entrepreneur Book Series

Publisher

JD-Biz Corp

P O Box 374

Mendon, Utah 84325

http://www.jd-biz.com/

Read more books from

Printed in Great Britain
by Amazon

44880077R00025